Contents

Before rugby – bando and cnapan

Rugby is a fairly modern game. We have only been playing it here in Wales for a little over a hundred years. But there were interesting games in Wales before rugby started being played. Usually the games were held on holidays: on New Year's Day, for example, and on 'mabsant' holidays – days that celebrate local saints. Two of the most popular games were **bando** and **cnapan**.

Bando was very similar to today's hockey and was popular in Glamorgan until the end of the nineteenth century. Two teams of players used sticks to hit a ball towards the goal. Sometimes hundreds took part, and people sustained nasty injuries. People used to play bando in places such as on the big beach behind where the Port Talbot steelworks are today.

Cnapan is perhaps the game that most resembles rugby. Cnapan was the name for the wooden ball, about the size of a cricket ball, that was used in the game. It would be boiled a few days before the match so that it would become slippery and difficult to catch. Usually, there were two groups of players from two different parishes. Sometimes the church gates in the two parishes served as the two goals, and these could be miles apart! Although some men – usually gentlemen – would be on horseback, most of the players were on foot – hundreds, and sometimes thousands. There is no mention of rules for playing cnapan, so it was a very rough game, and many of the players got injured or even killed. The ball would be kicked and thrown and there would be 'scrums' and 'line-outs' as the different teams tried to get hold of it. Big strong players similar to rugby forwards fought for the cnapan, and fast players, similar to rugby backs today, ran with the ball.

Pembrokeshire is famous for cnapan matches. Even though the tradition ended a long time ago, games were played between the parishes of Newport and Nevern as recently as 1985 and 1995. A hotel in Newport called 'Cnapan' is a reminder to us of the popularity of the game locally.

Chapel and church people were strongly against cnapan and bando because a lot of drinking and gambling occurred during the games. They believed that the games were a bad influence on ordinary people and began to arrange other events in the chapels and churches to attract people away from the games. So, slowly, the games came to an end.

Cnapan matches used to be held during the old New Year (January 12th) between the gates of Llanwenog and Llandysul churches in Ceredigion. As many people were killed or injured, the vicar of Llandysul decided in 1833 that the playing of the game should come to an end. He began another competition between the two parishes, a competition to test their knowledge of the Bible. This still takes place every year on January 12th.

The beginnings of rugby playing

It is said that rugby began in 1823 at Rugby School in England. According to the story, while playing football a boy called William Webb Ellis ignored the rules and caught the ball in his arms and started to run with it.

This story appeared for the first time in 1876 after William Webb Ellis died. Even though there is some doubt that it is a true story, Webb Ellis is still remembered. The name of the Rugby World Cup trophy is the Webb Ellis Cup; Ellis Park is the name of the rugby stadium in Johannesburg in South Africa, and there is also a plaque to commemorate him at Rugby School.

More details on William Webb Ellis are available on the website http://en.wikipedia.org/wiki/ William_Webb_Ellis

Some of the boys at Rugby School wrote down rules for the game in 1845. These are the first rugby rules to be written. Although other people played similar types of 'football', it was 'rugby football' that became popular because the rules were available.

Soon rugby spread very quickly to many other countries around the world. Between 1870 and 1920 rugby unions were established in England, Scotland, Ireland, Australia, South Africa, New Zealand, France, Rhodesia (Zimbabwe today), Argentina and Fiji. By now, many other countries, such as Canada, Namibia, Romania, Austria and Spain, play rugby.

The history of rugby in Wales

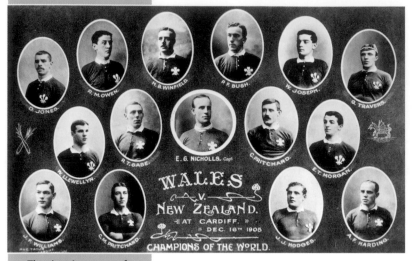

The victorious team of 1905. Search for the player wearing the cap. See page 63.

Saturday afternoons free, in addition to Sundays. Many villages and towns therefore set up a rugby team. Rugby offered field positions that were suitable for all kinds of players – it didn't matter whether you were tall or short, stocky or thin – so it was an excellent village game and brought a community together; everybody knew somebody who played for the team. People felt passionately about the game, and the competition between local village teams was fierce. There was also a new railway network to take supporters from place to place.

By the 1850s something similar to rugby was being played at Lampeter and Llandovery colleges. By the end of the 1870s there were teams in several towns in south Wales: Neath (the first to be formed, in 1871), Llanelli, Swansea, Newport and Cardiff. The teams were established by middle-class men who had played rugby at college. But before long, the game became popular with the working class.

The Industrial Revolution was having a great effect on Wales at the time. Many people had moved to the south Wales valleys and were looking for physical activities during their leisure hours. Also during this period, the workers started to have

Even though the new game had rules, fighting still occurred between the players and supporters. This is not surprising as breweries sponsored the clubs, the local pub was where teams changed before and washed after matches, and the supporters also drank beer during matches. In 1897, the Arms Park in Cardiff was closed for five weeks because supporters had attacked the referee. At the turn of the twentieth century, around 20,000 spectators would watch the main rugby club matches in Wales, many more than the football matches of the time.

Early team names

Some of the early Welsh teams were the 'Troedyrhiw Searchlights' and the 'Dowlais Harlequins'. The terrifying names for two teams from Carmarthen were the 'Diamond Skull Crackers' and the 'Shin Slashers'.

St Fagan's Village Rugby Team, 1901-02

'The devil's game'

Chapel people saw rugby as 'the devil's game'. Indeed, towards the end of the 1800s, chapelgoers in the Tawe Valley cut down rugby posts. During the religious revival in 1904-05, many rugby players became religious and burnt their rugby shirts. Jenkin Thomas from Kenfig Hill said, 'I used to play as a fullback for the devil, but I'm now forward for God'.

The **Welsh Rugby Union** was established in 1881 for a match against England. England won easily and refused to play against Wales the following year. But rugby developed quickly and Wales won the **Triple Crown** for the first time in 1893 (beating England, Scotland and Ireland).

As the players of England and Scotland were bigger and stronger, the Wales rugby players had to be different. They needed to nurture skills, think swiftly and run deceptively fast. This tactic succeeded and the Welsh rugby team won the **Triple Crown** six times between 1900 and 1911, losing only 5 matches out of 43. They also succeeded in defeating New Zealand 3–0 in 1905, the only team from Britain to do so during the All Blacks'

tour of 32 matches. There were 47,000 watching that fast, tough match. This is when Wales became famous for playing rugby. This was the first Welsh rugby **Golden Era**.

Willie Llewellyn's shop

Willie Llewellyn was one of the Welsh team's heroes in 1905. He was a pharmacist who had a chemist's shop in Tonypandy. In 1910, during the south Wales miners' strike, there was a riot in Tonypandy. Thousands of strikers rushed into the town breaking shop windows and stealing provisions. But the rioters refused to vandalise one shop – Willie Llewellyn's!

After a break in playing between 1914 and 1918 because of the First World War, the Welsh rugby team did not enjoy much success. In the 1920s, industry in Wales was also going through a difficult period because of the recession, with thousands losing their jobs. Thousands of people left Wales to look for work in other countries.

Most of the Welsh rugby team players were miners or steelworkers. During this period, one in every three men worked underground in the south Wales valleys. They were familiar with heavy work and were tough enough to play a physical game like rugby. They would work through the week like everybody else before going to play rugby on Saturday afternoons. Playing on an open field would be literally a breath of fresh air after working in unhealthy conditions underground or in the heat of the furnace.

The players were not paid whilst playing **rugby union**. But **rugby league** had developed in the north of England and players earned money for playing. 'Scouts' from the north of England would come to south Wales looking for new players and offering good money. During the recession, Wales lost many talented

Tongwynlais Rugby Team, 1922-23

international players to rugby league.

Many did not have much choice because they had lost their jobs. But they would never be able to play rugby union again because the rugby union people hated rugby league.

The Welsh rugby team had a successful period between 1950 and 1953, winning two Grand Slams and beating New Zealand in 1953. By the 1960s, there were fewer miners and steelworkers playing for Wales because many coal mines and steel works had closed. There were several teachers in the team during this period.

A memorable first cap

In 1967, when Keith Jarrett was only 18 years and 11 months old, he had an extremely memorable first match for Wales against England at Cardiff Arms Park. He scored 19 of the total points in the 34–21 victory! His kicking was superb – 5 conversions and 2 penalties – and he succeeded in scoring a try by running deep from his own half along the wing. "He can't miss, this laddie," said Bill McLaren, the Scottish commentator, on television.

At the time, players had to find their own way home. So, after the game, Keith Jarrett had to catch the bus back to Newport. But the Welsh supporters wanted him to join them in celebrating the victory. By the time he arrived at the bus station, the last bus had long gone. But the bus station manager insisted that one of his drivers took him home in a double-decker on his own so that he was left in peace!

The Golden Era of the 1970s

There was another golden era for Welsh rugby during the 1970s. For those watching rugby in the 70s, there will never be such a team! Even though they would sometimes begin matches badly, the team could move up a gear, especially in the last quarter of a match, and score memorable tries.

Here are some of the Welsh rugby team's achievements between 1969 and 1979:
- winning nine out of ten matches against England
- beating Australia three times
- winning the Grand Slam three times
- winning six Triple Crowns (including four in succession: 1976, 1977, 1978 and 1979)
- winning the Championship nine times.

Why were they so successful? The Welsh squad trained together, which was something very new at the time. Also, from the 1971-72 season onwards, a try was worth 4 points rather than 3 points (this changed to 5 points during the 1992-93 season). This favoured the Welsh team because they liked to handle the ball. Wales scored 105 tries between 1969 and 1979, 67 of them at the Arms Park.

JPR Williams

1971-72

60p

Edited by
GORDON
ROSS

BARRY JOHN
'Player of the Year'

Wales get the Grand Slam in a great year

Graham Price, Bobby Windsor and Clive Williams

9

Gareth Edwards

There were many world class players playing together regularly during this period. They were instinctive players able to read the game well. So they were able to adapt and react in an instant to what was happening on the pitch.

It is well worth watching a video or DVD to see the talents of the 1970s Golden Era team. Some of the most famous backs of the period were Gareth Edwards, Barry John, Phil Bennett, JJ Williams, Ray Gravell, JPR Williams and Gerald Davies. Gareth Edwards, Gerald Davies and JJ Williams scored a total of 49 tries between them. Some of the most famous forwards were Delme Thomas, Mervyn Davies, Derek Quinnell, Barry Llywellyn and the Pontypool front row: Charlie Faulkner, Graham Price and Bobby Windsor. Many of the Welsh team players during this period played for the Lions as they were the best in Britain.

Groggs of 1970s players

Barry John in Cardiff Arms Park

Gareth Edwards

People from all parts of the rugby world know about Gareth Edwards. He is considered to be one of the best rugby players ever. He was born in 1947 and brought up in Gwauncaegurwen, near Pontardawe. His father, Glan Edwards, was a miner. When he was a child, Gareth liked all kinds of sport. He would often play on 'Archie's field', a field belonging to a local farmer by the name of Archie, with his friends that included Huw Llywelyn Davies, the rugby commentator.

The PE teacher, Bill Samuels, at Pontardawe Secondary School was a huge influence. He mentored and trained Gareth Edwards to play football and rugby to a high standard. Gareth got a scholarship to Millfield public school, a school that specialised in sport.

In 1967, Gareth Edwards won his first cap for Wales as a scrum-half (number 9) when he was 19 years old. That first match was held in Paris, and he remembers eating steak and chips before the match and being allowed to keep the ball to remind him of his first cap. The following season, he became the Welsh captain at the age of 20, the youngest ever. He went on to win 53

Gareth Edwards' last try for Wales

GARETH EDWARDS

caps and scored 20 tries for Wales during the 70s Golden Era. He played for Wales with outside-halves such as Barry John and Phil Bennett. He was also very successful on the Lions' tours to the Southern Hemisphere. He was a member of the victorious tour of 1971 when the Lions won the series against the New Zealand All Blacks (for the first time) and in South Africa in 1974 when the Lions won every match.

What made Gareth Edwards such a special player? He was strong and fast and was able to make deceptive runs to beat the defence. He could read the game perfectly and was master of the grubber kick or the kick to touch. He developed the modern pass – the torpedo pass that spins in the air. He was also a very confident player, determined to win every match and score tries from all parts of the pitch.

Gareth Edwards retired from playing rugby in 1978 but he still contributes to S4C commentaries during international games. There is a statue of him in the St. David's shopping centre, Cardiff.

There is information on Gareth Edwards at:

www.sporting-heroes.net/rugby-heroes (English)
www.100welshheroes.com/cy/biography/garethedwards (Welsh only)

After the 1970s

The Welsh rugby team's extremely successful period continued until the beginning of the 1980s, but then other international teams began to play well. Wales nearly lost to Japan in 1983. Wales came third in the first World Cup competition in 1987 by beating Australia.

An enormous kick!

In February 1986, in the match between Wales and Scotland, Paul Thorburn kicked the longest penalty goal ever at the Arms Park – 70 yards and 8 inches, which is about 64 metres, a lot further than the halfway line!

During the 1990s, many international players left to play rugby league in the north of England. It was a difficult time for Welsh rugby. Wales got the **Wooden Spoon** in 1990 and 1991. Wales even lost to Western Samoa at the beginning of the World Cup competition in 1991. Many people wanted rugby union to become a professional game and this happened in 1995. Some of the rugby league players then came back to play for Wales.

Wales enjoyed a good period before the World Cup in 1999, winning 10 successive matches, but the team lost in the quarter finals.

Jonathan Davies, who played rugby union and rugby league at the very highest level

A disastrous game

In April 1998, Wales suffered an embarrassingly bad defeat against France, losing 0–51. This was the first time that Wales failed to score in 73 matches against France. Every one of the Welsh back-row were Swansea club players – and every one of them was given a yellow card. The French were ecstatic – they scored seven tries!

In the 2003 World Cup, Wales lost to England and New Zealand in two exciting and close matches.

2005 Grand Slam

Wales tasted success again in 2005 when they won the Grand Slam for the first time since 1978 and the Triple Crown for the first time since 1988. Mike Ruddock, the coach, was keen for the Welsh players to play an open game in order to show their talents.

The first match was at home against England. Shane Williams scored a try for Wales, Gavin Henson tackled strongly against Matthew Tait, but Wales were still trailing 8–9 with only a few minutes to go. Then Wales were given a penalty kick and Gavin Henson stepped forward to take it. It was a long kick of 44 metres and close to the right touchline, but Henson was confident and the ball flew between the posts. He later said: "I knew I could kick it, I'd been kicking them all week." Wales won 11–9 and everybody was thrilled.

Gareth Thomas and the team celebrate

Stephen Jones kicking

Wales travelled to Italy for their second match. Wales had lost in Italy for the first time in 2003, so everybody was quite nervous. But there was no need to worry, Wales scored six superb tries and won fairly easily by 38 to 8.

The third match at the Stade de France against France was very close; France were leading 15–3. But Stephen Jones kicked a penalty for Wales and the score was 15–6 at half time. During the second half, Martyn Williams scored two memorable tries, but France got a successful drop-kick to bring the score even at 18–18. Stephen Jones kicked a penalty (18–21) and a drop-kick (18–24). France needed a converted try to win and even though Wales had to defend vigorously towards the end of the match, they succeeded in retaining their advantage and won the match!

Tom Shanklin and Shane Williams

Gavin Henson breaches the England defence

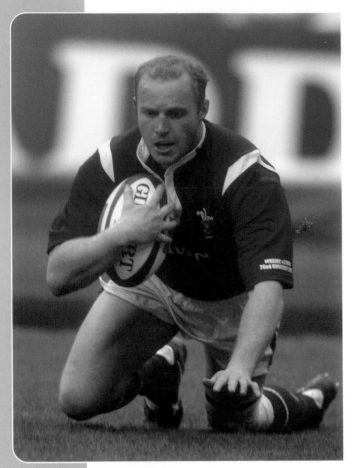

Martyn Williams

Groggs of the 2005 Grand Slam team

Around 40,000 supporters travelled from Wales to the fourth match against Scotland at Murrayfield. Scotland had just lost three matches but Wales' confidence was high. Wales attacked, immediately scoring tries; within a few minutes they were 19 points ahead! Try followed try – 6 in total! At one point the score was 3–43 before Scotland scored three tries of their own in the second half to bring the score to a more respectable level (22–43) for the home team. Some believe that the first half was the best 40 minutes of open rugby the Welsh team have ever played.

The Welsh team had only six days' rest before the fifth match – the final one – against Ireland at the Millennium Stadium. Both teams were competing for the Triple Crown. Because Ireland had lost against France, only Wales had any hope of winning the Grand Slam. It was a close match during the first half; Ireland took the lead early on with a penalty kick, but Wales hit back with a drop-kick by Gavin Henson. The prop, Gethin Jenkins, scored a try after he charged down an O'Gara kick, booting the ball over the try-line. Both teams then got penalties, and Gavin Henson kicked a penalty from 52 metres. At half time, it was 16–6 to Wales. During the second half, there were more penalty kicks for Wales. Kevin Morgan scored a surperb try after Tom Shanklin found a gap and the score increased to 29–6. Even though Ireland hit back with two tries, Stephen Jones succeeded with a further penalty kick, so the final score was 32–20. Over the duration of the five matches, Stephen Jones himself had scored 57 points and Wales had won the Grand Slam for the first time in 27 years!

Look for 2005 team's history in English on the website:

http://news.bbc.co.uk/sport1/hi/rugby_union/international/
http://www.telegraph.co.uk/sport/
and in Welsh on the following website:
http://www.bbc.co.uk/cymru/chwaraeon/archif/rygbi/rhyng/

Welsh rugby after 2005

Since then, the Welsh team have had mixed results with many of their key players sustaining injuries. There were some close matches against the Southern Hemisphere teams in the autumn series, but a number of disappointing matches, like the one against Scotland in February 2007 when Wales lost 21–9 at Murrayfield. But the present coach, Gareth Jenkins, is confident that things will come together by the 2007 World Cup.

You can see pictures of Welsh matches over the last few years on: www.welshrugbypics.co.uk and the most recent news about the Welsh rugby team at www.wru.co.uk

10 quick facts about the history of Welsh rugby

1. 126 miners have played for Wales between 1883 (Arthur Jones) and 2000 (Garin Jenkins).
2. Wales lost by 13 tries, 7 conversions, and one dropped goal to nil against England in the first match in 1881.
3. The best score for Wales so far has been Japan 0, Wales 98 in 2004.
4. The worst score for Wales so far has been South Africa 96, Wales 13 in 1998.
5. Wales have won 18 Triple Crowns, 9 Grand Slams and the Championship outright 23 times.
6. Neil Jenkins holds the record for scoring the most points for Wales – 1,049 points and the most points in one match – 30 against Italy in 1999.
7. Dwayne Peel is the youngest player to win 50 caps for Wales – he was 25 years old when he achieved this in February 2007.
8. Nobody has won more caps for Wales than Gareth Thomas – he has 94 in total (June 2007).
9. Phil Bennett was the first ever substitute to come onto the pitch in a Welsh game.
10. Michael Owen is the 1,000th player to play for Wales.

Neil Jenkins

Gareth Thomas

Essential numbers:

- **2** teams of **15** players aiming to score tries and kick goals.
- A game of **80** minutes: **2** halves of **40** minutes.
- Half time of **10** minutes between the two halves.
- **5** points for a try, **2** points for converting a try and **3** points for a successful penalty kick or drop goal.
- The kicker has **1** minute to take a penalty kick or convert a try.
- **1** referee and **2** linesmen are responsible for managing the match.
  Sometimes there is a **4**th referee – a video referee.
- As many as **7** substitutes can be on the bench, up to **2** substitute forwards and up to **5** other substitutes.
- **7**-a-side rugby is also popular, with international competitions held in Dubai and Hong Kong every year.

The Team Every one of the **15** players in each team has specific work to do.
Usually, the team is divided into two groups:

Forwards (numbers 1 to 8)

- The forwards are the 'pack' and they are the ones who form the scrum.
- The *front row* are numbers 1, 2 and 3.
- The *second row* are numbers 4 and 5.
- The *back row* are numbers 6, 7 and 8.
- Traditionally, the forwards were stronger, heavier and slower than the backs.
- In the modern game, it is expected that the forwards are big, strong *and* fast.

Backs (numbers 9 to 15)

- The *half-backs* are numbers 9 (scrum half) and 10 (outside half).
- The *three-quarters* are numbers 11, 12, 13 and 14.
- The *full-back* is number 15.
- The link between the backs and the forwards is number 9, the scrum-half
- Traditionally, the backs were lighter and faster than the forwards
- By today, the backs need to be fast *and* very strong.

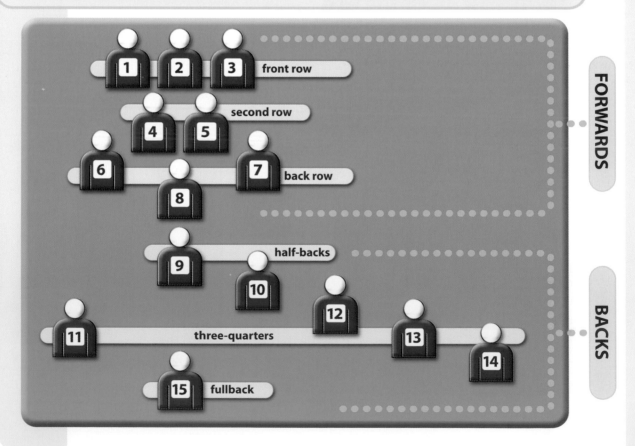

Each team member's duty

Each member of the team needs tackling and defending skills.

So they must:

- Be very fit
- Deal easily with the ball (passing and kicking)
- Tackle strongly
- Read the game well.

But each member of the team has specific tasks as well.

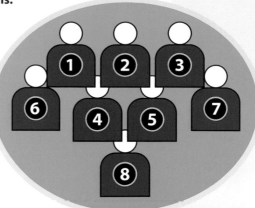

THE SCRUM

1 Loose-head prop forward
3 Tight-head prop forward

- Keeping the scrum steady
- Taking the main weight in the scrum with the rest of the pack
- Assisting the other forwards in the line-out.

> **Look out for:**
> **Gethin Jenkins** (The Blues and Wales) and **Duncan Jones** (The Ospreys and Wales) and his curly blond hair. **Duncan** and **Adam Jones** (The Ospreys and Wales) are known as the 'Hair Bears'.

> **Ask about:**
> **Barry Llewelyn** (the 1970s)
> "He was a forward before his time, strong but also fast," says Alun Wyn Bevan.
> **Graham Price** (1975 until the beginning of the 1980s) – a member of the 'Pontypool front row' (with **Bobby Windsor** and **Charlie Faulkner**. He toured once with the Lions as well as winning two Grand Slams and taking part in three Triple Crowns with Wales.

Duncan Jones

2 Hooker

- Throwing the ball to the line-out – this is a very important skill
- Hooks the ball in the scrum and directs it back towards the back row.

> **Look out for: Matthew Rees** (Llanelli Scarlets and Wales).

> **Ask about: Bobby Windsor** (the 1970s). Steel industry worker. One of the 'Pontypool front row' that became famous in the 1970s for their free and lively play and for precision throwing at the line-out.
> **Garin Jenkins.** A miner who played frequently for Wales in the 1990s.
> **Robin McBryde.** The hooker from Menai Bridge who now coaches the Welsh team's forwards.

Garin Jenkins

4 and 5 Lock

- Jumping or supporting other forwards as they jump in the line-out to win the ball
- Adding weight to the scrum
- Channelling the ball in the scrum away from the hooker towards the back-row.

> **Look out for:**
> **Ian Gough** (Gwent Dragons and Wales) and **Alun-Wyn Jones** (The Ospreys and Wales).

> **Ask about:**
> **Delme Thomas** (the 1970s), Llanelli captain when they won against New Zealand in 1972. An excellent jumper in the line-out.
> **Robert Norster** (the 1980s), played for Cardiff and Wales.

Alun-Wyn Jones

6 Blindside flanker

7 Openside flanker

- Pushing in the scrum
- Jumping or supporting the other forwards as they jump in the line-out to win the ball
- Getting hold of the loose ball – usually number 7 is faster than number 6
- Tackling strongly
- Carrying the ball.

> **Look out for:**
> **Martyn Williams** (Cardiff Blues and Wales). He also has a brown belt in judo!
> **Jonathan Thomas** (The Ospreys and Wales).
> **Alix Popham** (Llanelli Scarlets and Wales).

> **Ask about:**
> **John Taylor** (end of the 1960s/beginning of the 1970s). His nickname was 'Basil Brush' because of his bushy hair and beard. He played for London Welsh, Wales and the Lions. The ultimate flanker, solid tackler, effective in the ruck and maul, and a fast runner.

8 Number-eight

- Controlling the back of the scrum – getting the ball to the scrum-half
- Jumping or supports other forwards as they jump in the line-out
- Carrying the ball
- Big tackler.

Ryan Jones

> **Look out for:** **Ryan Jones** (The Ospreys and Wales).
> **Ask about:**
  Mervyn Davies (end of the 1960s until the mid 1970s). One of the best number-eights that Wales ever produced. Captain of Wales and the Lions. "**Mervyn Davies** had arms like an octopus. You'd think you'd got past him, but then he would catch you." (Ray Gravell).

Dwayne Peel

9 Scrum-half

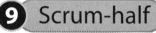

- Putting the ball in the scrum
- Picking up the ball from the base of the scrum
- Ensuring quick service to the backs
- Good kicking – e.g. along the wing, to the corner, or a high kick into empty space for the winger to pursue
- Ensuring play continues after a maul or ruck

> **Look out for:**
  Dwayne Peel (Llanelli Scarlets and Wales). Started playing rugby for Tumble under 8s club.
  Michael Phillips (The Ospreys and Wales).

> **Ask about:**
  Gareth Edwards – Gareth Edwards is considered to be one of the best-ever players.

Turn to the item about him on pages 11 and 12.

10 Outside-half

- Key position for controlling the game
- Kicking – usually, the outside-half takes the set penalty kicks
- Making strategic decisions as he attacks and puts the ball in gaps in the opposition defence so that other players cross the gain-line.

> **Look out for:**
> **Stephen Jones** (Llanelli Scarlets and Wales), captain of Wales, a sound kicker who can control the game.
> **James Hook,** The Ospreys' and Wales' new star.

Barry John

> **Ask about:**

Barry John and **Phil Bennett** (the 1970s). "Phil Bennett could create space, and Barry John could create time." (Ray Gravell). Barry John was called the 'King [of the Lions]' after the successful tour in 1971.

Jonathan Davies (the 1980s). He was a successful rugby union and rugby league player at the highest level. By now he is a television commentator.

Neil Jenkins (the 1990s). An extremely successful kicker. He won 87 caps and scored 1,049 points – a record for Wales. He is currently a kicking-coach for Wales.

11 and 14 Wingers

(11) left and (14) right wingers

- The team's 'greyhounds', the fastest runners
- Speeding with the ball for the open ground/the corner and scoring tries
- Carrying the ball over the gain line
- Whilst defending, forcing the other team's players to cross the touchline.

> **Look out for:**
> **Shane Williams** (The Ospreys and Wales).
> "He's like quicksilver." (Ray Gravell)

> **Ask about:**
> **Gerald Davies** (the 1960s and 1970s), one of the best attacking wingers ever seen. He scored 20 tries and played 46 times for Wales.
> **JJ Williams** (the 1970s). He was an athletics sprinter for Wales and was one of the fastest wingers of his time. He played for Bridgend, Llanelli, Wales and the Lions.
> **Ieuan Evans** (the 1990s). Scored 33 tries for Wales and was captain 28 times.

Shane Williams

12 and 13 Centres

(12) inside and (13) outside centres

- Creating space and carrying the ball across the gain-line whilst attacking
- Delivering the ball quickly to the players to the outside
- Making sure that there are no gaps in the defence for the opposition to attack.

> **Look out for:**
> **Tom Shanklin** (Cardiff Blues and Wales).
> **Gavin Henson** (The Ospreys and Wales).

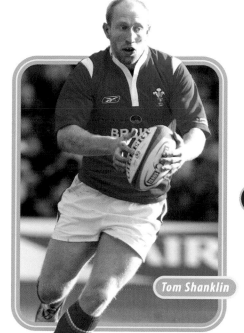

Tom Shanklin

> **Ask about:**
> **Bleddyn Williams** (the 1940/1950s), 'The Prince of Centres'.
> **Ray Gravell** (1970s) A powerful centre; several players would often be needed to tackle him. He played with all his heart for Llanelli, Wales and the Lions.
> **Scott Gibbs** (the 1990s). A fierce tackler and powerful runner. He scored a memorable try for Wales when the team beat England by one point in 1999.

15 Fullback

- The last line of defence
- Making sure that the ball gets to the forwards – usually by kicking
- Reading the game and placing himself in the correct position on the field
- Joining in the attack to create space and possibly giving the attack a different direction
- Sometimes acting as an additional outside half

> **Look out for:**
> **Kevin Morgan** (Gwent Dragons and Wales).

> **Ask about:**
> **JPR Williams** (the 1970s). A strong and fearless fullback. He would turn defence into attack and was an adept kicker. He was also a talented tennis player. After retiring from international rugby, he continued to play throughout the 1980s and 1990s.

You can look for information on many rugby players on the wikipedia website: en.wikipedia.org

Kevin Morgan

23

THE MAIN ELEMENTS

These are the basic elements and rules of rugby played by over 19s. Some rules are different for younger players.

Scrum

A scrum is needed to restart play. Only the eight forwards of the two teams are allowed to be in the scrum. After the forwards have formed the scrum, the scrum-half places the ball in between the two teams. The two sets of forwards push against each other and the hooker directs the ball back with his heel. The scrum-half must move around the scrum to pick up the ball and either pass or kick it.

The forwards of one team may be heavier than their opponents, but this does not mean that they will be better at scrummaging. The forwards use a scrum machine to practice this.

Because players can sustain severe injuries to their necks if the scrum collapses intentionally, the referee will penalise this aspect strictly.

Maul

At least three players are needed to form a maul. The players must stay on their feet and close in on the player who is holding the ball. A maul comes to an end if the ball falls to the ground, or if the ball or the player carrying the ball comes away from a maul. After this a scrum will be called.

Ruck

Two or more players can form a ruck. They have to stay on their feet and close in on *the ball that's on the ground* between them. If there is no way of playing the ball in a ruck, a scrum will be called.

Line-out

A line-out will takes place after the ball goes over the touchline. So the purpose of the line-out is to get the ball back into play. At least two players from both teams need to be in a line-out. The team throwing the ball in decides how many players should be in the line-out. The teams form two parallell-lines 5 metres from the touchline with a gap of 1 metre between them.

The player throwing the ball in (the hooker usually) stands on the outside of the touchline. He must throw the ball in straight without stepping over the touchline. The ball must travel at least 5 metres before it is caught or falls to the ground.

Endless line-outs!

The game between Scotland and Wales at Murrayfield in 1963 was very boring. Wales won by getting one successful penalty kick and drop goal; the final score was 0–6. But everybody will remember the game because there were **111 line-outs** during the game! The scrum-half and Welsh captain, **Clive Rowlands**, kept kicking into touch!

Losing because of a line-out

It was a close game between Wales and New Zealand in Cardiff in 1978. With Wales leading 12–10 towards the end of the game, a line-out was formed. As the ball got thrown-in, two of New Zealand's players, **Frank Oliver** and **Andy Haden**, cheated. Both jumped out from the line-out in order to make the referee think that Welsh players had pushed them out. The referee blew his whistle, and gave New Zealand a penalty kick. **Brian McKechnie** succeeded with his kick and Wales lost, 12–13.

Handling the ball

Players pass, knock or hit the ball to each other. The ball must travel backwards when it is being passed by hand from one player to the next.

Knock-on

Players 'knock-on' the ball by losing the ball (e.g. in a tackle) or failing to catch the ball. Sometimes the ball hits a hand or arm and goes forward. A scrum occurs if the ball is knocked on accidentally. But the referee will give a penalty kick to the opposition if the ball is knocked on intentionally.

Try

The other team's try-line must be crossed and the ball planted in the try area in order to score 5 points. It is also possible to score by grounding the ball on the try-line. In international games and some important games between clubs if the referee is unsure, the video referee will give his verdict on whether the player has grounded the ball successfully.

England's **Leo Price** scored the quickest try ever (after 10 seconds) in the game against Wales in 1923.

Gareth Thomas holds the record for scoring the highest number of tries for Wales – 35 tries in all (June 2007).

Mark Taylor scored the first ever try in the Millennium Stadium in June 1999 when Wales beat South Africa 29–19 for the first time ever. Because the stadium was not ready there was only room for 27,000, but the Wales supporters made plenty of noise!

11 memorable tries

1. Gareth Edwards against Scotland, 1972.
He ran from a distance evading the defenders, grubber-kicked, grounded the ball and slid into the mud at the edges of the Arms Park. His face was covered in mud!

2. Scott Gibbs against England, 1999.
Wales won the ball from the line-out, it went from Robert Howley's hands to Scott Quinnell and then to Gibbs. Scott Gibbs sidestepped past England's tacklers and went for the try-line, helping Wales win by a hair's breadth – 32 to 31.

3. Kevin Morgan against Ireland, 2005.
Tom Shanklin broke through the midfield defence and passed the ball to Kevin Morgan who crossed the try line to ensure Wales won the Triple Crown and the Grand Slam.

4. Adrian Hadley against England, 1988.
Hadley went on to score a scissors with Mark Ring before crossing the try line and Wales won at Twickenham, 3–11.

5. Barry John against England, 1969.
Barry John went on one of his trademark zig-zagging runs across the pitch and changed speed brilliantly before scoring.

6. Ieuan Evans against England, 1993.
Emyr Lewis kicked the ball on. Rory Underwood for England hesitated while trying to retrieve it, without realising that Ieuan Evans was galloping up behind him. Evans kicked the ball on, sped past the England fullback, Jonathan Webb, and dived on the ball for a memorable try. Neil Jenkins converted the try and Wales won 10–9.

7. Ken Jones against New Zealand, 1953.
Clem Thomas crosskicked the ball perfectly for Ken Jones to catch it and fly past two of the New Zealand defenders by the posts. A key try during the final seconds, the last time Wales beat New Zealand (13–8).

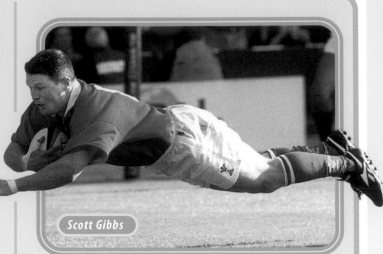

Scott Gibbs

8. Scott Quinnell against France, 1994.
Quinnell won the ball from the line-out and charged like a bull towards the try-line. Scott's father, Derek, had scored a similar try against Scotland in 1978.

9. Phil Bennett against Scotland, 1977.
The backs of the 70s Golden Era were at their best, zig-zagging across the pitch deep from their own half. The ball went from JPR Williams, to Steve Fenwick and then to Gerald Davies who sped ahead before passing the ball to Phil Bennett. Bennett passed to David Burcher, who passed inside to Fenwick again. Fenwick passed the ball with one hand to Bennett, and he sidestepped past the defence, sped on and scored under the posts. This was the try of the season when Wales won the Triple Crown for the 14th time.

10. Charlie Faulkner against Ireland, 1975.
As the match neared the end, Graham Price, another member of the Pontypool front row, passed the ball to Faulkner and he ran for the line. The try was an extremely popular one even though the game had already been won.

11. Martyn Williams against France, 2005.
Martyn Williams' try came at a key moment of the game when France were leading 15–6. Stephen Jones broke through the defence and passed the ball to Shane Williams. He passed back inside to Martyn Williams. With a conversion by Stephen Jones the score was 15–13 and Wales were back in a match which they won in the end.

Kicking

Players can kick the ball instead of passing or running with it. When attacking, the player will kick in order for his team to keep possession of the ball after it has landed. When defending, the players kick the ball over the touchline in order to gain ground and get the chance to gain control of the ball back from the line-out.

Place-kick

Whilst taking a place-kick the ball is positioned on a mound of earth before kicking. The ball can also be placed on a piece of plastic called the tee, or on a mound of sand or sawdust. A place-kick can either be the conversion of a try or a penalty.

Drop-kick

In making a drop-kick, a player drops the ball to the ground and kicks it into the air as it hits the ground. The drop-kick starts the match or restarts the match after the other team has scored. The player can also use a drop-kick to kick the ball over the crossbar between the posts to score 3 valuable points during play.

Wales lost to Ireland at Lansdowne Road in 1968, and the score was Ireland 9 Wales 6. But it could have been worse for Wales – the referee gave Wales 3 points for Gareth Edwards' drop goal that flew at least a foot beyond the post!

Grubber-kick

The player drops the ball to the ground and kicks it as it rebounds. But the grubber-kick skims or bounces across the ground instead of rising into the air like the drop-kick. When the opposition are close to the kicker, the grubber-kick is useful to get the ball between them.

Free-kick

A team gets a free-kick if the opposition has infringed or if a player has called for a **mark**. It is not possible to score from free-kicks but kicking in any direction is allowed. The other team have to back away 10 metres from the kicker. As soon as the kicker kicks the ball, the opposition can rush forward.

2 important conversions

Wales against Scotland at Murrayfield, 1971.
Wales were behind, 18–14, and with only a few minutes to go. Wales won the ball from the line-out, and it went along the line to Gerald Davies. He succeeded in scoring a try – 3 points at that time – so it was now 18–17. Gerald failed to plant the ball under the posts, so the conversion was a difficult kick for John Taylor from the right-hand touch-line. Taylor was a left-footed kicker and as everybody held their breath, he kicked the ball perfectly between the posts to give Wales a 18–19 victory.

Wales against England at Wembley, 1999 – it was a 'home' game for Wales whilst the Millennium Stadium was being built. England were in the lead 25–31 with eight minutes to go when Scott Gibbs scored a brilliant try. Now, the score was 30–31, and it all depended on Neil Jenkins' conversion. He had already succeeded with 6 penalty kicks and 1 conversion, but this was the most important kick. Nobody was surprised when Jenkins' kick succeeded, and Wales won, 32–31. After the previous year's whitewash (England 60, Wales 26), Wales were ecstatic!

Penalty-kick

When taking a penalty-kick, the kicker may choose between a drop-kick, a place-kick or a grubber-kick. The team can also choose a scrum instead of taking the penalty-kick. After being awarded a penalty-kick, the kicker may choose to score three points with a drop-kick or place-kick. Another option is to gain ground by using a drop-kick or grubber-kick for other players to follow the ball or that the ball is kicked upwards over the touch-line.

Players must try not to concede penalties because the match can be won or lost with points scored from penalty-kicks. If the other team concedes penalties, it's important that you have a good kicker in your team.

Memorable penalty kicks

The Wales match against France, at the Arms Park, 1972, was the last match played by Barry John, 'The King'. He decided to give up rugby, at the age of only 27, after a sparkling career. He kicked an impossibly long penalty kick, 54.8 metres, and Wales secured a victory of 20 points to 6.

In 1993, Neil Jenkins scored 8 penalty goals but Wales lost 24–26 against Canada. One of the most memorable penalty kicks is the 44 metre kick by Gavin Henson against England in 2005. The score was 8–9 to England, but Wales succeeded in winning by 11 points to 9 thanks to Henson's kick in the final minutes of the game. After winning this match, Wales went on to win the Grand Slam.

THE PITCH
Length and width
Rugby is played on a grass pitch (and sometimes on mud!).
The pitch can be up to a 100 metres long and 70 metres wide.

The posts
In the middle of the two try lines, there are posts in the form of an 'H'. The two uprights are 5.6 metres apart joined by a crossbar 3 metres from the ground. A kick is successful if the ball goes over the crossbar and between the posts. Even if the ball is higher than the posts themselves, the kicker is still successful.

dead-ball line

try line

10-metre line

halfway line

22-metre line

touchline

try area

up to 100m

up to 70m

Lines
There are two lines twenty two metres from each try line. There are another two lines ten metres either side of the centre line. There are also lines across the pitch five metres from the two touch lines. Beyond the try line (twenty two metres at most) is the dead-ball line.

Flags
There are 14 flags on the pitch: a flag on each of the four corners of the two try lines and the two touchlines, one on either side of both 22-metre lines, one on either side of the halfway line and one on each corner of the try areas.

Some rules involving the pitch
- As the match starts on the halfway line, the ball must reach the other team's 10 metre line unless one of the opposition plays it first.
- When scoring a try, the ball must be grounded in the try area (between the try line and the dead-ball line).
- If the ball is touched down in the try area by a defending player or it rolls over the dead-ball line, the game restarts on the 22-metre line.
- Throwing the ball deliberately over the touchline is not allowed. The referee gives a penalty kick to the opposition if this happens.
- In line-outs, the forwards at the throw-in must be at least 5 metres from the touchline.
- If a player catches the ball in his own team's 22-metre area, he can call 'a mark'. A mark must be called for immediately upon catching the ball. The opposition must step back 10 metres, and the player is allowed to kick the ball without any opposition player challenging him.

Kit

Shirt, shorts and more

Usually teams wear long-sleeved shirts with a collar and cotton shorts. The shorts were much longer in the early days than they are today. The socks go up to the knee and the top of the socks are turned down.

In a match, the two teams must wear shirts that are obviously different from each other. For example, when they play away, the Welsh team wear grey shirts when the opposing teams also wear red shirts. Usually, there are numbers on the back of the shirts and often the players' surnames appear above the number. Some companies sponsor rugby teams and so their logos also appear on the teams' shirts.

As well as the usual kit, players can wear shoulder pads, a mouthguard to protect their teeth and an ankle support. The forwards can wear a scrum cap. But wearing anything that could injure other players, such as rings, zips, buckles or clips, is not allowed.

Dwayne Peel modelling the Welsh kit

The Welsh kit in 1911

The kit worn by Cardiff in 1900

29

Rugby boots

In the 19th century, rugby players wore the ordinary worker's heavy leather boots. The boots were high in order to protect the ankle. By today, the backs wear low rugby boots so that they can run faster, and the forwards wear sturdier boots. It's important that rugby boots protect the foot as players often tread on each other's feet.

Usually, there are six studs at the front of the rugby boot and two under the heel. The studs must be secured to the boot and shorter than 18mm. Short studs are ideal on hard and dry pitches but on muddy pitches, long studs are better. Having a single stud at the front of the boot is not allowed. The referee makes sure that there are no sharp dangerous edges to the boots in case of injury to players.

Leather and synthetic material are used in today's boots. The leather can stretch to fit the player's foot snuggly, but when it becomes wet, the boot can lose its shape. Boots made of synthetic material are cheaper and lighter. It's important to choose boots that fit well to avoid blisters. Boots must be looked after by cleaning and keeping the leather or the synthetic material in good condition.

JAMES HOO[...]
WALES 200[...]
AUTUMN
ITERNATIO[...]
BOOTS

Rugby balls

When boys first started playing rugby at Rugby School in the mid 19th century, William Gilbert, a cobbler in Rugby, made the balls for the school. He used a pig's bladder with leather casing around it. Some unlucky person had to use a clay pipe to blow the bladder up when it was green and smelly.

The first balls were round and larger than the balls of today. In 1892 the standard size of the ball was decided upon and the insides made of rubber instead of bladder. The oval ball developed because it was easier to hold when running. Of course, because the ball is oval shaped, it moves differently on the ground to a football.

These days the ball must weigh between 400g and 440g. The circumference of the ball must be between 760mm and 790mm in length and between 580mm and 620mm in width. The ball must also have four panels.

The ball used to be made of leather, which would become heavy if it got wet. But then at the beginning of the 1980s, synthetic materials began to be used. The modern rugby ball keeps its shape whatever the weather. It is made of polyurethane, synthetic leather, laminated polyester, latex and glue.

The name of one of the early rugby clubs in Wales was 'Rhymney Pig's Bladder Barbarians'.

The great clubs of the past

Delme Thomas celebrates beating the All Blacks in 1972

Before 2003, the important clubs in Wales were Llanelli, Swansea, Cardiff and Newport. Countries such as Australia and New Zealand used to play against these clubs as well as against the Welsh rugby team when they toured. Neath, Bridgend, Pontypridd and Pontypool were also famous clubs.

Here are some of the old clubs' great victories:

• **Swansea 11 New Zealand 3 in 1935** – Haydn Tanner and his cousin Willie Davies were the Swansea half backs; both were 18 years old and in their final term at Gowerton County School. After the match, the New Zealand captain, Jack Manchester said, "Haydn Tanner and Willie Davies gave brilliant performances. Tell them back home we were beaten by all means, but please not by a couple of school kids!"

• **Cardiff 8 New Zealand 3 in 1953** – Bleddyn Williams was the Cardiff captain on the day. He also succeeded in defeating the All Blacks in a Wales shirt.

• **Llanelli 9 New Zealand 3 in 1972** – Llanelli rugby club were celebrating their centenary in 1972. Delme Thomas, the captain, led his team onto the pitch after hearing the coach Carwyn James from Cefneithin saying that he was confident they could win. The most memorable try of the match was when Phil Bennett hit the crossbar with his penalty kick, one of the New Zealand players caught the ball and kicked it but Roy Bergiers was there to charge the ball down and score the try that won the match.

• **Against Australia** – Cardiff have played against Australia six times and have beaten them every time! Llanelli and Swansea beat the Australian team in 1992. At the time, they were the World Champions!

• **Newport's successes.** Between 1957 and 1974 Newport beat Australia, New Zealand, South Africa and Tonga.

In Wales today, 293 clubs form part of the Welsh Rugby Union. There are four regional clubs, 14 clubs in the Premier League, and the rest of the clubs in leagues on five levels.

Websites to access more information about the clubs:

www.swansearfc.co.uk/whites.php
www.llanellirugby.com/history/
www.cardiffrfc.com/index.cfm?method=rugby.history
www.blackandambers.co.uk/
www.neathrugby.co.uk/CLUB-HISTORY.html
www.ponty.net/club/index.php
en.wikipedia.org/wiki/Pontypool_RFC

WELSH RUGBY REGIONS

● **Llanelli Scarlets**
west, mid and north Wales

● **Swansea Neath Ospreys**
Swansea, Neath, Maesteg
and Bridgend area

● **Cardiff Blues**
Cardiff and the Glamorgan valleys

● **Gwent Dragons**
Newport and the Gwent valleys

www.answers.com
www.scarlets.co.uk
www.newportgwentdragons.com
www.cardiffblues.com
www.ospreysrugby.com

The rugby regions of Wales were created in 2003. Originally, there were five regions but the Celtic Warriors (Pontypridd and Bridgend areas) came to an end in 2004. Many people were very unhappy when the regions were created. It was easy for some regions – for example the Llanelli Scarlets followed on naturally from Llanelli rugby club. But it was more difficult for the Swansea, Neath and Bridgend teams to come together to form the Ospreys and for Pontypridd supporters to start supporting the Cardiff Blues. Some people still find it difficult to support their local region's team because they miss their old clubs.

The four regional teams represent Wales in the Celtic League, the Heineken Cup and the EDF Energy Cup. So far, the Welsh Regions have not made their mark in Europe, but the Scarlets have won the Celtic League once, and the Ospreys won the title for the second time at the end of the 2006-07 season, the only region to achieve this so far. The Ospreys also beat Australia 21–6 in November 2006.

The best club players in the lower leagues move up to play for their regions. Each region has an Academy for young players between 15 and 19 years of age. They receive fitness training, nutrition advice, psychological skills etc. so that they can become professional players for the region later on. But instead of keeping them 'safe' within the Academy, the regions want them to gain experience by playing 'proper' rugby every Saturday for a club from the lower leagues. In this way young players develop leadership skills and learn lessons by making mistakes along the way.

Llanelli Scarlets

Stradey Park is the home of the regional Llanelli Scarlets team and the Llanelli Premier League rugby team. The capacity is 10,800. Rugby has been played there since 1879.

Many memorable matches have been played at Stradey Park. Llanelli beat Australia in 1967 and New Zealand by 9–3 in 1972.

The Scarlets and Llanelli rugby teams are planning to move to a new stadium on the outskirts of Llanelli. The land at Stradey Park will have to be sold for development in order to raise money to build the new stadium.

Matthew Rees

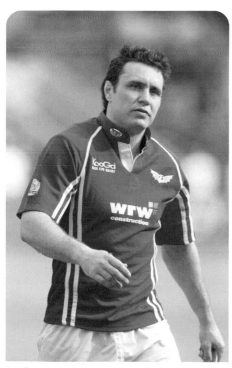

Stephen Jones

Alix Popham

Swansea Neath Ospreys

Liberty Stadium is a few miles east of the centre of Swansea city. This is the area where there was heavy industry in the past. On this site, the Morfa Copper Works and the Glandŵr Silver Works operated up until the mid 1920s.

The stadium holds over 20,000 people. It was opened in 2005. It is home both to the Ospreys regional rugby team and Swansea City football team. So up to 60 football and rugby matches are held there each season.

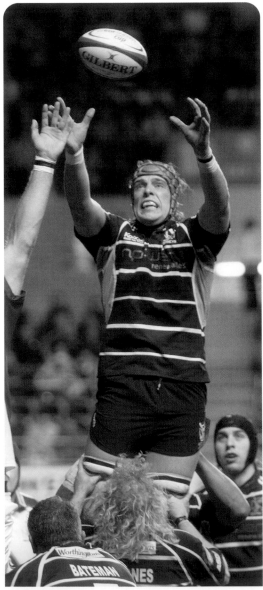

James Hook

Adam and Duncan Jones

Alun-Wyn Jones

Cardiff Blues

The old Arms Park was home to both the Welsh team and Cardiff Rugby Club on two separate pitches. Whilst the regional team, the Cardiff Blues, still play on the club pitch, the Welsh rugby team now play their international matches at the Millennium Stadium. Robert Howley scored the last try for Wales at the Arms Park.

Ray Gravell has very fond memories of watching rugby with his father at the Arms Park and of playing there for Wales:

"The experience of coming down through the tunnel with the other players was amazing. You could see the light at the other end. As you ran on to the field, the deafening noise and all the faces in the crowd really hit you. I felt as if I was growing in size, turning into some kind of 'superman'."

In 1969, the Arms Park was extended. The old north stand was pulled down. There was only room for a crowd of 29,000 on the other three sides of the pitch. In fact, the stadium was a building site, with workmen still working on it whilst the matches went ahead!

Chris Czekaj

Xavier Rush

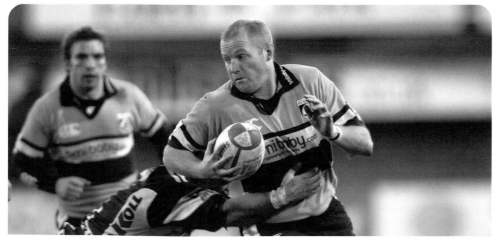

Martyn Williams

Gwent Dragons

NEWPORT

GWENTDRAGONS

Rodney Parade stadium is home to the Gwent Dragons and Newport rugby team. Rugby and other sports have been played there since 1877. The stadium's capacity is 11,700.

Colin Charvis

Ceri Sweeney

Michael Owen

Local clubs

Below the regional clubs, there are 14 clubs that play in the Premier League (*the Principality*). Below the Premier League are all the other Welsh clubs in five leagues (*Asda*) according to area.

Your local club will play matches in one of these leagues. Depending on size, your local club will have the following teams:

- first team
- second team (or development team)
- under 19s youth team
- a number of teams for children and young people – from an under 8 team and up to 16 years of age
- women's rugby team.

Many people work voluntarily for the local clubs. They coach, assist, run the bar, wash the kit or are officials on the club's committee. Many of them are former players with the clubs.

Local companies sponsor clubs by buying kit and clubs will often raise money by holding special evenings. Indeed, a rugby club can be the focus of social life in many areas in Wales.

So, if you'd like to play rugby outside school, there will be a warm welcome waiting for you at your local club.

Women's rugby

Is rugby only a game for men and boys? Not at all. This used to be true, but by now girls and women get the chance to play in teams at every level.

There are about 1,500 women playing rugby regularly. There are 25 senior women's clubs. Girls under 12 years old can play in mixed teams. After this there are teams for girls under 14, under 17 and senior girls' teams. The best women progress to the Welsh squad and play for their country.

Catrin Evans is the secretary of the Dolgellau women's rugby team. She organises matches for the women's team:

"Rugby is the most popular sport for women in north Wales. It's an energetic game and is great for letting off steam."

Timeline for Women's rugby

1970s – women started to play rugby.

1983 – the Women's Rugby Union was established in Wales and England.

1986 – women from Wales played in the first international match – the Great Britain team against France.

1987 – the first game between women from Wales and England.

1991 – the first Women's Rugby World Cup competition is held.

1995 – establishing home internationals between the countries of the British Isles: Wales, England, Scotland and Ireland.

2001 – the six nations competition established between Wales, England, Scotland, Ireland, France and Spain. Now there is a team from Italy playing instead of the Spanish team.

Wales' women against Ireland, 2007

One of the players from the Dolgellau rugby team, Elen Evans, plays as a fullback for Wales:

"I began playing rugby for the Dolgellau senior women's team when I was 16 years old. By now, I often play for Wales. The rules are exactly the same as men's rugby, but the big difference to the men's game is that women's rugby is an amateur game.

So I work during the week and travel to south Wales on Friday night in order to train over the weekend. Sometimes there will be an international match on Sunday and a crowd of three or four hundred people come to see us. Playing for Wales is an awesome experience every time."

Ysgol Dyffryn Conwy, Llanrwst, girls' team

Elen Evans running with the ball

There is information about Welsh women's rugby, including reports on the matches and so on at www.wru.co.uk

Key people

Players

Rugby has been a professional game since 1995. But only around 140 players are totally professional. These are the players at the highest level who play for the regions. The players in the Premier League are paid some money but also need to have other jobs. The players at the lower levels get a small fee but rugby is a hobby for them, not a living. Indeed, many players pay into their clubs and raise money for them in order to have the pleasure of playing.

The dream of every Welsh rugby player is to win a cap and wear the red shirt for Wales. Here is one Welshman who has succeeded in doing just that.

Nicky Robinson's questionnaire

Club: Cardiff Blues
Position: outside-half
Place of Birth: Cardiff
Date of Birth: 3 January 1982
Height: 6 foot 1 inch
Weight: 14 stone 8 pounds
Primary school: Ysgol Melin Gruffudd, Cardiff
Secondary school: Ysgol Gyfun Glantaf, Cardiff
Most memorable game: Playing for Wales against Argentina in Buenos Aires in 2004.
International caps up to May 2007: 13

A week in the life of Nicky Robinson

Monday: Everybody does weightlifting in order to strengthen the body – it's important to be in good shape to play the game. At lunchtime, we eat together as a team, we eat healthy food. We play a game of cricket, which is a lot of fun, during the lunch hour.

Tuesday: We watch videos of our opponents to see what kind of game they play and what the team's weaknesses are. There's rugby practice after that because it's important that each member of the team understands his role. As an outside-half it's important that I practice my kicking, so I stay on later in order to concentrate on that.

Wednesday: Rugby practice again. Again, I practice my kicking for an hour or two after that. Some afternoons we have community duties. Today we're coaching school children. The whole squad enjoys meeting their young fans.

Thursday: A rest day today. Rugby is a very physical game so it's important that the body is given a chance to rest. Even on my day off I practice kicking. After that, usually, I meet some of the boys for coffee in town. Sometimes, we have to work for the club. Today, I am modelling the Blues' new clothes for the shop catalogue. Doing this kind of stuff is fun.

Friday: The day before the match we have a 'team run', where all the boys who will be playing have one last training session. We work out the moves and tactics we intend to use against our opponents. I practice my kicking for the last time before the match.

Saturday: The day of the big match. I don't eat much before the match because I have to make sure my body is at its best before playing.

Psychology is also very important; we have to be very focused before going on the pitch. After the match the two teams meet and eat together. Rugby is a great way of getting to know people and making new friends.

Sunday: The day after the match I tend to relax. I enjoy many different sports and enjoy watching football or playing golf. I also have Sunday lunch with my family. They're very supportive of my rugby career.

The team captain

The coaching team (see page 44) decide who should be the team's captain.

They look for someone who is:
- a regular member of the team
- able to speak well (very often, the captain is the one who has the last word before going onto the pitch)
- able to lead by example
- a hard worker on the pitch
- an inspiration to other players
- the embodiment of the club's values.

As **Ray Gravell** says:

"A captain should not ask anything of anybody that he would not be willing to do himself."

Ray Gravell remembers **Delme Thomas**, Llanelli captain, speaking before the famous match against New Zealand in 1972:

"Delme said that he would be willing to sacrifice everything that he had accomplished in the world of rugby to win that afternoon. And that he would not want anyone else, only those who were in that changing room, with him to face the All Blacks."

His team was inspired by his words, and they won 9–3.

Sometimes, it's difficult for a player to deal with being a captain. Some players don't play as well after being chosen as captain. So the coach has to rethink and choose another captain.

Here are some of Wales' best captains: **Bleddyn Williams** – the last captain to lead Wales to victory against New Zealand in 1953.

Clive Rowlands – he was captain every time he played for Wales – 14 times in all.

John Dawes, **Mervyn Davies** and **Phil Bennett** – Wales captains during the Golden Era of the 1970s.

Some recent captains: **Ieuan Evans, Robert Howley, Scott Gibbs, Gareth Thomas, Stephen Jones**.

The Welsh captain in the match between Ireland and Wales in Belfast in 1914 was the Rev. J. Alban Davies. But there was nothing reverential about this match. The nickname for the Welsh pack was 'The Terrible Eight', and many of the players spent their time fighting when they didn't have the ball. The match was remembered in Ireland as 'The Roughest Ever'.

Mervyn Davies

Phil Bennett

Robin McBryde, Wales forwards' skills coach

Rowland Phillips, Wales defence coach

Nigel Davies, Wales attack coach

The coaching team

The national team and the regions have a group of specialist coaches:
- Head coach/director of rugby
- Forwards/backs coaches
- Attack/defence coaches
- Fitness coaches
- Skills coach
  (with the national team)
- Nutritionist

Clubs in the lower leagues also have several coaches – e.g. head coach, fitness coach, forwards/backs coaches – who coach the first team and the development team.

One of the main roles of the coaches is to decide on the direction of the team's training. Each time the team plays, a video will be made of the game. The video is analysed and they discuss different aspects of their play. For example, what percentage of the possession the team got, how many tackles were lost, how many times and how did the team win the line-outs and so on. Also, individual feedback is put together for each player in the team – this is called '*sports coding*'. At the end of this process the coaches can analyse each example of scrums, mauls, rucks, line-outs and open play. They will also have clips of individual players tackling, passing, kicking or running with the ball.

Before each game, the coaches will also look at an analysis of the opposition's matches so that each player knows what to expect from the team as a whole and from individual players.

Head coach / director of rugby

This is the most important person in the coaching team. He needs to inspire the players to achieve their best form in each match and throughout training during the week. The best coaches;
- bond the squad together
- treat each player fairly
- understand the strengths and weaknesses of each individual
- listen to players' ideas
- set realistic targets
- understand psychology and how to inspire people.

Wales was the first country ever to have a coach. David Nash was the first Wales coach in 1968. The team began to meet on Sundays to practise before international matches. Previously, the Welsh team had a manager on tour, but the captain decided what the tactics were, and the team members met each other for the first time about 48 hours before each match.

Lyn Jones, head coach of the Ospreys

Gareth Jenkins

(Welsh coach from May 2006).

"A coach who succeeds in inspiring everybody he coaches. He is full of enthusiasm for rugby and is passionate about the sport . . . He is an emotional and brave person, and players are willing to follow a person who is willing to show bravery and emotion." (Alex Lawson)

"A passionate and emotional person. He is extremely thorough and analyses every aspect of play. A very intelligent character. He is proud of his country and the Welsh boys respond to that." (Ray Gravell)

Mike Ruddock

(Welsh coach between 2004 and February 2006, including the Grand Slam in 2005).

"Mike Ruddock was essential in passing on the element of Welshness to the players. He made them realise that we are different to everybody else. He knew his Welsh history and raised the team's understanding of our history by talking about Llywelyn and Glyndŵr." (Ray Gravell)

Graham Henry

(Welsh coach between 1998 and 2003).

"As a man from New Zealand, maybe Graham Henry wasn't as emotional as some of the Welshmen who had coached Wales. But his way of thinking and attitude was right – winning at all cost. And winning convincingly." (Ray Gravell)

"Even though he had a run of 10 matches without defeat with Wales, in the end he did not fully understand the Welsh character. He tried bringing things that worked in New Zealand into the Welsh game. But the tradition of the game in Wales was different, and the Welsh boys (at the time) were smaller in size than the New Zealand boys. So Henry's game felt unnatural to the Welsh because it relied more on power than on skill." (Huw Llywelyn Davies)

John Dawes

(Welsh coach between 1974 and 1979).

Wales won 4 Triple Crowns in succession in the four years 1976–79 and two Grand Slams in 1976 and 1978 under his leadership.

"John Dawes had been captain of the Lions and won the series against New Zealand in 1971. Even though he was not one of the most outstanding players, he was well respected and could do the basics properly. And to cap it all, he knew how to treat people well." (Huw Llywelyn Davies)

Clive Rowlands

(Welsh coach between 1968 and 1974, the youngest ever to be a coach for his country).

"A Welshman through and through. A passionate patriot. He was master of using psychology, passionate and very vocal in the changing room." (Ray Gravell)

"Clive Rowlands holds a very special record in world rugby – he has held every post possible – he played for his country and was captain and coach for the national team, he was a selector and chairman of the selectors, president of the Welsh Rugby Union and manager of the Lions. And he also did all this against New Zealand. He has even sung in a choir before a New Zealand match!" (Huw Llywelyn Davies)

Gareth Jenkins

Mike Ruddock

Graham Henry

Clive Rowlands

Carwyn James

(Llanelli coach in the 1970s and the Lions in 1971).

Carwyn James never coached Wales, but he was one of the most influential coaches that Wales ever had. Gareth Jenkins, Wales' head coach, and Ray Gravell played in the Llanelli team when Carwyn James was coach. Carwyn James also coached for a period during the end of the 1970s in Rovigo, Italy, thereby helping to develop rugby in Italy. The Carwyn James Centre is located at Gwendraeth Secondary School; he was a hero in the area. The sports building at the University of Wales Aberystwyth is also named after him.

"Carwyn was a genius – in several fields. He knew people as individuals and knew how to get us playing at our best. He made me think I was a better player than I really was. Once, he said to me, 'Raymond, you'll represent your country.' I began to believe that, and that's what happened in the end. He had a special presence. He was quiet but confident in the changing room and could criticise in a very constructive way." (Ray Gravell)

www.sportstat.co.uk/mediaguide/CarwynJames.html

Alex Lawson at work

Fitness coach

The fitness coach's work is to condition the players physically to play a rugby match. The players' aerobic fitness must be improved (so that the player's body makes better use of oxygen). Also the players must become stronger and faster.

The fitness coach creates a programme of exercises appropriate for rugby. This includes:

- strength and power exercises – weightlifting, dragging weights – up to 100 per cent of the body weight – forwards and backwards
- speed exercises – sprinting
- flexibility exercises – stretching
- jumping exercises, hopping and jumping (*plymetric training*)
- other exercises (*cross-training*), e.g. swimming, ball games with balls of different sizes.

According to Alex Lawson, who is fitness coach with the Swansea Neath Ospreys, these exercises greatly benefit players' bodies:

"The effect of fitness training on young players (under 19 years old) is amazing, as they are still growing. Also, older players can improve their performance greatly. By becoming fitter, they can play at their best for 80 minutes. But the player himself must make the effort and sacrifices. The fitness coach only creates the programme for them."

Nutritionist

The Welsh team have a nutritionist who creates a diet programme for all the international players. Four times a year, the players will be body-fat tested. They will also be blood and saliva tested. After analysing the results of these tests, the nutritionist can create a detailed programme for each individual player.

The programme focuses on:
- the player's food intake
- the kinds of food he eats
- how often he eats during the day
- the percentage of protein, fats and carbohydrates he should eat
- any supplements the player should be taking
- hydration (how much liquid the player drinks)

Every professional player is expected to follow the programme carefully so that he can play at his best.

AN EXAMPLE OF A PROFESSIONAL RUGBY PLAYER'S MENU FOR A TYPICAL DAY

Breakfast: Eggs (and/or bacon) (*protein*), cereal and toast (*carbohydrates*)

Lunch: Chicken (*protein*) and pasta/rice/potatoes (*carbohydrates*) or steak (*protein*), jacket potatoes (*carbohydrates*) and vegetables (*fibre*). Carbohydrates are needed every time before training.

After training: 'Protein shake' – powder mixed with milk or water.

Snack: Jaffa cakes to give a quick release of energy.

Supper: Large steak (*protein*) No carbohydrates are needed because no training is done after supper. Protein is important to replenish the body.

Liquid: A player is weighed before and after training. Straight after training, he must drink between 1 and 2 litres of water for every 1kg he has lost through training (around half a kilogram is lost for every hour of training).

NO smoking and **VERY LITTLE** alcohol – after a match with food only.
Alcohol makes the body dehydrate (losing too much water).

Medical officer

The Wales rugby team has a medical officer who gives the players general medical advice.

If a player sustains an injury, the medical officer will look at the video of the match at the point where the injury took place in order to see exactly what happened. He will then have a look at the X-ray slides and talk to the player and the physiotherapist in order to create a recovery programme.

If injuries happen frequently in any one aspect of play, he then informs the Welsh Rugby Union. After this the Union will consider if there is a need to change the rules so that fewer injuries occur.

Physiotherapist

Every one of the main teams has a physiotherapist. Their work is to help players recover from injuries. When players sustain an injury during a match, the physiotherapist runs on to the pitch to give him first-aid.

If the player cannot play after sustaining the injury, the physiotherapist creates a programme of exercises specifically for that part of the body which received the injury. This can include stretching exercises, body massage and so on. Different types of exercise will be needed to recover from different injuries.

Some injuries take time to get better, so a player has to be patient. It's important that players don't start playing again too soon after getting injured. Doing so could do a lot of damage. Sometimes players have to retire from the game if they suffer the same injury time after time.

Ospreys physiotherapy staff

Groundsmen

The groundsmen's work is extremely important. Without it, it would not be possible to hold a rugby match. The groundsman is responsible for the maintenance of the pitch so that the grass is in ideal condition.
So, he must:
- spread fertiliser on the ground so that the grass grows well
- water the pitch in hot weather
- make sure that the ground drains if it is very wet
- cut the grass
- sow seeds if the grass gets thin
- get rid of weeds
- mark the lines
- set out the posts and flags
- pick up rubbish.

The groundsman has something to do all year round. In the summer, before the rugby season starts, the rugby posts need painting. Also, he must make sure that all the lines are marked correctly on the pitch. After the season has started, some parts of the pitch will get muddy. He will need to make holes in the ground with a fork and put in some sand to help the pitch dry. Sometimes new turf will have to be put down to replace bad patches.

The most modern pitches, e.g. the Millennium Stadium, have an underground heating system that prevents the pitch from freezing during the winter. Also, there are systems available that show if the pitch needs watering and indicating its temperature.

A match in a sand-pit

Every rugby match had been cancelled on 4 January 1998 – all apart from the match between Neath and Llanelli. Three tons of sand was put on the pitch and the match went ahead!

Frozen solid

The winter of 1962-63 was very hard and rugby pitches would freeze solidly. But the groundsmen at the Arms Park insisted that the match between Wales and England in January 1963 would go ahead. They put down a thick layer of straw some days before the match, removed most of it on the morning of the match, leaving a thin layer to be removed an hour before the match. The match went ahead after the workers had cleared the ice and snow from the terraces.

Officials

Linesmen

There are two linesmen on the pitch. They stand either side of the pitch, behind the two touchlines. If the ball goes over the touchline, they raise their flags and stand where the ball went over. When a player kicks at goal, the linesman will stand beneath the posts and decide if the kick was successful. The linesman has to keep an eagle eye out for any foul play. If they see a player throwing a punch or kicking, they have to contact the referee.

Even though there are two linesmen, they do not have the last word. The referee takes the final decision every time.

Referee

The referee is the person who controls the game and makes sure that the players follow the rules. He (or she) keeps time and records the score. There are video referees in international matches and in some important matches between clubs that are televised. The video referee will look carefully at any incident on video, e.g. a disputed try, and relay his decision to the referee on the field.

Some referees begin refereeing in their teens. But, usually, players decide to start refereeing in their twenties.

There are plenty of courses available. The Welsh Rugby Union organises courses for referees at different levels, but every referee must follow the International Rugby Board's Level One course. After taking more courses and gaining experience, it's possible to referee matches between teams at higher levels. The most important thing is to read *Welsh Rugby Union: The Rules of the Game*, the referee's 'bible' – it includes all the laws of the game. Alun Wyn Bevan, the rugby

commentator, used to referee. Here is his list of what every referee needs:

- detailed knowledge of all the rules
- the ability to deal with the 30 players under his control
- plenty of humour, and being willing to laugh
- must be totally fair and honest
- must be very fit in order to keep up with play
- a referee must acknowledge if he makes a mistake – it's easy to make mistakes with 30 people on the field, and 16 of them (forwards) close together
- the referee must remember that the players are the most important people on the pitch and not himself.

The international referee Nigel Owens from Pontyberem adds:

"When players of each team come to shake hands at the end of the match, I know that things have gone alright. They have enjoyed the match, and that's important."

Nigel Owens also talks about the pressure on a referee during a professional match:

"These days, people's careers can depend on decisions taken during a match. If a team loses because of one of the referee's decisions, it could mean a coach losing his job or a

Alun Wyn Bevan refereeing

Nigel Owens

player being dropped from the team. So it's important that each decision is correct."

For Alun Wyn Bevan, it was easier to referee big matches rather than less important ones:

"When there are 25,000 watching a match, the noise of the crowd is background noise. But when there are 50 people watching, the referee hears everything they say. And if they disagree with the referee, they can say awful things!"

So referees can feel very lonely. According to Nigel Owens, the coaches and players of the two teams are great friends before the match, but after the game, one team will be disappointed and become withdrawn. Having said this, referees get to travel to different places and meet many different people.

Commentators

If you can't get to matches yourself, commentators bring them to you live on radio or television.

The first English-language commentary on a Welsh rugby match was heard on British radio in 1927, when Wales played against England at Twickenham. During the Second World War there were two English-language sports commentators on the Welsh Home Service – G.V. Wynne-Jones and Alun Williams.

In the 1950s Eic Davies from Pontardawe was the first to give Welsh-language commentary on a rugby match. He created many common terms used today in Welsh, for example, *cic adlam* (drop-kick), *cais* (try), *ystlys* (touchline), *mewnwr* (scrum-half) and *maswr* (outside-half). By the 1970s his son, Huw Llywelyn Davies, provided regular radio commentary for international matches in Welsh. John Evans would co-commentate and Carwyn James would give his expert opinion. Some Welsh-speaking listeners would watch the match on television, turning the sound down to listen to the Welsh-language commentary on the radio.

Huw Llywelyn Davies

Clive Rowlands and Alun Wyn Bevan

It wasn't until the 1980s that rugby matches were shown on television with Welsh-language commentary and Huw Llywelyn Davies was the first to do this. By then, the Welsh-language terminology had been accepted.

"When I was a child, we used to play in Welsh but the terms were in English. But children today use terms like 'mewnwr' (scrum-half) or 'cic adlam' (drop-kick) totally naturally."

By today, there is Welsh commentary on most of the big rugby matches on S4C and Radio Cymru.

Popular commentators in the English-language on BBC Wales and Radio Wales are Gareth Charles and Nick Webb with ex-players such as Garin Jenkins, Phil Bennett and Jonathan Davies contributing to the commentary.

According to Alun Wyn Bevan, there is a big difference between commentating on radio and commentating on television:

"The secret on television is to know when to keep your mouth shut because much of the action is self-evident. But on the radio, you can talk and talk endlessly. You are the camera that creates the picture of the match for the listeners."

According to Huw Llywelyn Davies: "On the radio, it's important to say 'what' has happened. It's important to introduce the geography of the field so that the listeners can visualise it – who's moving in which direction. On television, you have to say 'why' things happen. The viewer sees it all, so unless you add something to the picture on camera, there's no point in saying anything."

Huw Llywelyn Davies will begin preparing some days before commentating on a rugby match:

"I find out who's playing and I collect statistics on the players and the game. I prepare a list of facts but I try not to push the statistics. They are there in case something happens on the rugby pitch. You don't need to mention that John Jones is a talented cricketer until he catches a difficult ball.

Of course, you have to learn the names of all the players. This can be difficult when teams from the South Sea Islands or Japan come over. But often it's more work to remember who's who when there are seven Joneses and several Williamses playing in a match! Seeing the boys train helps me recognise players and remember their names."

Ray Gravell with a young supporter

Poem

Mark Taylor's Try *(translated from Welsh)*
(against Japan, 9 October 1999)

The ball comes in to the crook of Craig's arm
who turns his back on Japan's men
like a castle wall,
as solid as the concrete of the stadium itself.

The Welsh captain takes the ball.
Scythes past the flanker.
Like a jet, he whizzes down the right wing,
halfway down the field, untouched by a single hand.

In the end it hits the ground.
Will it come back? The forwards dig for the ball . . .
Out it comes!

The dragon's backs handle the ball
like musicians in an orchestra,
until it gets into the fullback's hands.

Howarth is a fox in a red shirt.
On a zigzag path,
throwing his hand into the Japanese winger's face.
He does a clog dance
over the twenty two line.
Offers Bateman the ball
and then whips back suddenly
into the centre's path.

He clears the rest of the field like a combine.
Crosses the line.
Falls on the ball like a sack of potatoes.
The crowd is on its feet! Ogi! Ogi! Ogi!

Ysgol Capel Garmon

Supporters

Welsh supporters are extremely enthusiastic. It's easy to fill the Millennium Stadium when Wales are playing at home and an army of supporters travel with the Welsh team to the four corners of the world. It's a lucky person who has a ticket to watch Wales and an unlucky one who has an appointment with the dentist when Wales are playing.

The 2004-05 season, when Wales won the Triple Crown and the Grand Slam, was a very special one for Welsh supporters; 40,000 from Wales travelled to watch the international team play against Scotland in Murrayfield. During the 2005-06 season, Wales played seven home games at the Millennium Stadium and the stadium was full to capacity each time. Half a million people gathered there in all during the season.

The atmosphere at the Millennium Stadium is very threatening to any opposing team, with the Welsh supporters looking like a sea of red.

Singing your heart out

Singing has always been an important part of Welsh rugby. When the singing starts, the home team gets an added boost. Even if the Welsh team is losing, the Welsh supporters have to sing!

Here are some of the Welsh supporters' favourite songs when watching rugby:

- **Hen Wlad fy Nhadau (Land of my Fathers)** – sung for the first time as an anthem in 1905 during the match between Wales and New Zealand, as a response to the New Zealand 'Haka'. Recently, choirs and a number of stars such as Bryn Terfel, Tom Jones, Shirley Bassey and Katherine Jenkins have been singing the anthem before matches at the Stadium.
- **Calon Lân**
- **Cwm Rhondda** ('Guide me, O Thou Great Jehovah')
- **Sosban Fach** (even though this is really a Llanelli song)
- **Hymns and Arias** (a song by Max Boyce).

The Welsh supporters like wearing red and white scarves and hats, painting red dragons on their faces and some of the men like wearing the Welsh kilt. Often there'll be a huge leeks and daffodils in the crowd as well!

Before the match between Wales and England in January 1963, the pitch had frozen solid. So the crowd had to sing 'Hen Wlad fy Nhadau' without the team – it was far too cold for them to come out onto the pitch to stand still!

Charlotte Church, Max Boyce and Katherine Jenkins

Max Boyce

Max Boyce comes from Glyn-neath and he used to be a miner. He became famous after recording an evening concert live in 1973, 'Live at Treorchy Rugby Club'. The night included Max singing and telling stories about the valleys and rugby. It was an extremely successful night, with the audience really enjoying it, and before long, the recording of that evening became popular.

Max went on to record again, he reached number 1 in the album charts and got a gold disc. He has had television series with the BBC and has published books of his songs and poetry. He still holds concert evenings and takes part in pantomimes.

What is Max Boyce's secret? His songs, his stories and his poetry all involve the people of the south Wales valleys, Welsh rugby supporters and their feelings. For example, he sings ballads about closing the coal mines in the seventies and eighties and recounts funny stories about rugby supporters on tour. He's obviously a very likeable, warm character and can make people laugh easily. On stage he wears a Wales hat and scarf and a huge leek on his coat.

Reading the *Western Mail*

The *Western Mail* gives Welsh rugby a lot of attention. When there is an international match, the *Western Mail* publishes a special colour front cover. It includes photos and statistics of past matches against Wales and the opposing country, the latest information and opinion on the match to be played. After each match, there will be detailed analysis on the back pages of the paper and a chance also for readers to give their opinion on the team's performance and to choose their dream team for the next match.

The Millennium Stadium, Cardiff

This is Wales' main international playing field. The stadium opened in June 1999. Wales beat the South African team in the first main rugby match to be played there. Even though the stadium itself is fairly new, rugby has been played on the site (the Arms Park) since the 1870s. So there's a long tradition of playing and watching rugby there. It is one of the few international pitches located in a city centre; as a result, every time an international rugby match is held in Cardiff, the city itself becomes alive with supporters.

The stadium is amazing and the supporters – up to 74,500 people – feel that they're close to the play. If the weather is bad, the roof can be closed.

There are still problems with the pitch which is created from around 7,500 pallets of turf because concerts and other events are also staged at the stadium. During the winter, not enough light reaches the ground to allow the grass to grow and the surface breaks up easily. Special lamps are used to try and solve this problem.

Wales' Crown

(translated from Welsh)
(Poetry workshop at the Millennium Stadium, May 2001)

A strong castle,
protecting Graham Henry's boys;

UFO
the extra-terrestrial players;

A Big Mac Octodecker
gives us strength to express ourselves;

A Venus Fly-Trap flower
that crunches Dallaglio's bones;

A huge ear
that hears the anthem's heartbeat;

Preseli
that's full of the spirit of the old giants of yesteryear;

The dragon's cave
spitting flames;

A cruiser ship
taking the name 'Cymru' into the sunshine across the world

A watch
that tells us our time is nearly at hand . . .

Ysgol Arberth

Some of the other grounds of Wales

The Brewery Field, Bridgend
This stadium was the home of Bridgend rugby club before the reorganisation in 2003. Now this is the home of the rugby union team 'Bridgend Ravens' that plays in the Premier League. Rugby league matches are also played here.

The Racecourse, Wrexham
The Racecourse has been the home of Wrexham football team since 1872, but the Welsh team and Llanelli Scarlets have also played there. It has capacity for 15,500 spectators.

Sardis Road, Pontypridd
The home of Pontypridd rugby team.

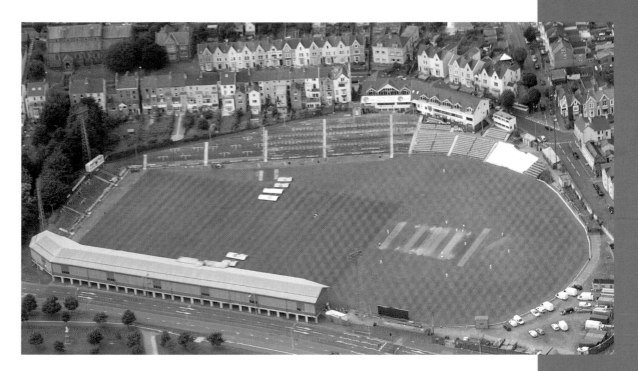

St. Helen's, Swansea

This is where Swansea rugby club play. In the past, all the big matches were played here – this is where Swansea beat New Zealand in 1935 and Australia in 1992. By now, the big rugby matches are played at the Liberty Stadium.

The Gnoll, Neath

The home of Neath rugby team.

Gren Cartoons

Gren (Grenfell Jones, 1934–2007) is famous for his cartoons of Welsh rugby.

Gren, originally from Hengoed, managed to create a new cartoon every day for 40 years for the South Wales Echo. His cartoons showed life in the imaginary village of Aberflyarff. There was a lot of humour in his work and sheep called Nigel and Neville carried funny messages on their woolly coats.

Gren loved rugby, and every year he would produce a rugby calendar for the most ardent of Welsh rugby supporters. He published 24 books and won a prize for being the best regional cartoonist in Britain four times in the 1980s. A board game based on Gren's characters is currently being developed.

What about copying Gren's style in order to create a cartoon of one of your favourite heroes?

Bleddyn

The supporter

Enjoying the game

The hooker

The lock forward

Conversion

Ponty and Pop

Groggs

Since 1965 John Hughes has been creating ceramic statuettes of famous people from the world of rugby and other sports. He first began in a shed in the garden, but soon moved to an old pub in Pontypridd where 'The World of Groggs' is today. When the Welsh rugby team had their success in the 1970s, people started to collect Groggs of their favourite players. By now, there is a vast collection of past and present players from which to choose.

Visit the website: www.groggs.co.uk

PHIL BENNETT

GERALD DAVIES

WILLIAMS

GROGG Shop

DUNCAN JONES

ADAM JONES

JAMES HOOK